Translations
of the Gospel
Back into
Tongues

SUNY POETRY SERIES
PAUL ZWEIG, Editor

Editorial Board
SHIRLEY CLAY SCOTT and C.K. WILLIAMS

Translations of the Gospel Back into Tongues

poems by
CD Wright

State University of New York Press, Albany

Published by
State University of New York Press, Albany

Printed in the United States of America

For information, address State University of New York Press, State University Plaza, Albany, N.Y., 12246

Library of Congress Cataloging in Publication Data

Wright, C. D.
   Translations of the Gospel back into tongues.
   (SUNY poetry series)
   I. Title. II. Series.
   PS3573.R497T7 1982   811'.54   82-17047
   ISBN 0-87395-652-4
   ISBN 0-87395-685-0 (pbk.)

Grateful acknowledgment is made to the following magazines in which these poems first appeared:

Akros: "Fields," "Boss Of Darkness," "Two Women Sleeping On A Stone"
Black Warrior Review: "The Substitute Bassist," "Alla Breve Loving," "Jazz Impressions In The Garden," "Who Sit Watch In Daylight," "from *Livelihoods Of Freaks And Poets Of The Western World*," "Landlocked, Fallen, Unsung"
Field: "Libretto," "Yellow Dresses," "Obedience Of The Corpse"
Invisible City: "Pontoons"
Ironwood: "Smoke Rings," "The Beautiful Urinals Of Paris," "Falling Beasts," "True Accounts From The Imaginary War"
The Little Review: "Run For The Roses"
Ploughshares: "Bent Tones"
Quarterly West: "The Secret Life Of Musical Instruments," "Blazes,"
raccoon: "Crescendo," "Wanderer In His Thirtieth Year," "White Shutters,"

Variants of "Tours," "Listening To A Brown-Eyed Man Play It For Somebody Else," "Alla Breve Loving," "Fascination," "Obedience Of The Corpse," "The Beautiful Urinals Of Paris," "The Night Before The Sentence Is Carried Out" appeared in the chapbook *Terrorism* published in 1979 by Lost Roads Publishers, Fayetteville, AR, out-of-print.

Anthologized poems from this selection are "Obedience Of The Corpse" printed in *OZARK, OZARK A Hillside Reader*, Miller Williams, ed., U of Missouri Press, 1981, and again in *Storie di Ordinaria Poesia, Poeti Americani degli Anni '70*, a cura di Riccardo Duranti Roma, Savelli, 1982. Also printed in *Storie di Ordinaria Poesia* from this selection, "The Night Before The Sentence Is Carried Out."

10   9   8   7   6   5   4   3   2

By CD Wright

Alla Breve Loving (1976)
Room Rented By A Single Woman (1977)
Terrorism (1979)

to Frank
for Kay Duvernet
and
for Cathy Fabacher

Contents

You must let me go first because I live in the sea always now, and know the road.

—*Emily Dickinson*

True Accounts From
The Imaginary War

1

Pontoons

When people dream they glide under the quilt,
Leave the pier.
When they wake up their bed is on the beach,
Their cover on the floor.

I can still see my brother
Floating alongside me
In the canopied bed,
His head falling back
Into the feathers of a childhood.

Our mother hovers over him like a moth,
Brushes his face.
The powder off her collar stays in the air.

Whatever happened to the women
My brother didn't marry,
The pale hair under their arms,
The nights he spent without them,
His enemies.

They would turn up again
So would his face in the basin,
White handkerchief on a mirror.

Scissors cut paper, rock breaks scissors,
Paper covers rock.

2

Drift

We are walking off the lands
We were raised on,
No combs or quilts handed down to us

The daughters of men cold as the Volga
Who drink in front of the fire and say —
Not another word out of you,

And of women who sit and pull at their shawls
Holding their tongue.

We die on a hard bed of snow
With our eyes half open like the door
Between a lighted room and the covered furniture
Of a soul.

The barn is dark and far
The moon odd as a monument;

Our hair falling out as hay from the loft,
Our skin sloughing off in scrolls,
Our hand in our underwear
The furthest pole.

3

True Accounts From The Imaginary War

We were on a boat and we were blindfolded.
We heard wind
Tear down the sailcloth and the moon
Wash up like debris.

Hundreds crossed the desert
Of their life on foot.
Folding money blew out of their sweatbands.
The dunes rose in their eyes.

Then the conquerors put everyone together.
Told us, Go below. We groped
Along a cold wall. We crawled.
We settled on a cobbled floor like rugs
Thrown from a balcony.

Some claimed we were in a tower.
Others swore it was a cave.
Hell is a pure faith.

Prisoners looked for our kin.
When the mainlander met the islander
In the dark she recalled her own wilderness.
She lay her ear on the other's brown belly,
Listened to the sea.

Night and all morning
The conquerors picked up broken bodies
Of light. The sun came up
Smoking behind the dunes in their eyes.

The eldest of us sang. The young did not.
They stroked their wild vines, their wet avenues.
They bled.

The islander gathered the mainlander
In her arms. She thought of markets,
Bars, cars passing the Opera.
She heard the jukebox in the jungle
And rain.

4

Two Women Sleeping On
A Stone

They were going to wade. The sun beat
Down. Before long they were over
Their head. Water dark and deep. Life after death
Aquatic. Like dreams and jazz its beaches
Are lush and cool. Transbluent.

This is the spot where a school of musical instruments
Washed up like men-of-war;
Performed for the love of ancients, fallen creatures,
And the law which passed unobserved.

The two we gave up for drowned, dropped
Their troubles like an anchor and listened,
Wringing their hair like the necks of beautiful birds.
They lay on a stone. One blowing
On the other's wounded foot. Fishermen trolling
Down the coast of their pain. They made for the trees.
Leaving bewildered tracks.

There are women in other ports
Who would not touch their meal tonight.
Let their mackerel shine in the moonlight, let it stink.
The women drink to their health, being friends.
Speak ill of their husbands, being drunk.
Admit they dreamed everything: the anemone's sting,
The source of all music, the long faithful marriages of the
    dead.

5

Foretold

Even in countries with the blackest eyes
Those with one blue one rule.
The bad doctor is respected, the well-witcher is not.
This is the dog's life.

With daylight
The called climb out of the hills under darkening
Loads. They lay their burdens down
Of an evening, snore like the wind.
Asleep, they know themselves
As the ones who fly.

To set foot on the desired land
All incurable dreamers must rise and go down
To the thirty-fifth latitude.

Approach the wide porches of the chosen
With ears laid back,
In accordance with the common law —
The baddest dog entitled one bite,
And as it has been written
Is better to die trying than not to die.

6

Bad Grounds

Somewhere else, before
There were so many graves to water,
Women fled the burning townships
With their smoky possessions.
Their veils flared, dissolving
In the limbs of eucalyptus.
The molten ring from their nose
They flung down wells, their hair in sheafs
To the threshing floor.
Under blurred stars
The unproven songs of their time were sung,
They slept as one
Overcome by the breathless dream
Of having reached the sea
Where the world begins, tomorrow.

7

Falling Beasts

Girls marry young
In towns in the mountains.
They're sent to the garden
For beets. They come to the table
With their hair gleaming,
Their breath missing.
In my book love is darker
Than cola. It can burn
A hole clean through you.
When the first satellite
Flew over, men stood
On their property, warm
Even in undershirts,
Longing to shoot something.
The mule looks down
The barrel of the gun,
Another long row to plow.
Bills pile up in fall
Like letters from a son
In the army. An explosion
Kills a quiet man.
Another sits beside a brass lamp
In a white shirt
And cancels his pay.
A thousand dulcimers are carved
By the one called Double Thumb.
Winter cuts us down
Like a coach. Spits snow.
Horses flinch
Against the cold spurs in the sky.
We look for the oak
Who loves our company
More than other oaks.
The loveliest beds
Are left undone.
Hope is a pillow
Hold on.

8

Tours

A girl on the stairs listens to her father
Beat up her mother.
Doors bang.
She comes down in her nightgown.

The piano stands there in the dark
Like a boy with an orchid.

She plays what she can
Then turns the lamp on.

Her mother's music is spread out
On the floor like brochures.

She hears her father
Running through the leaves.

The last black key
She presses stays down, makes no sound,
Someone putting their tongue where their tooth had been.

9

Deep Rivers
for Frances Mayes

A woman warms herself at a fire.
She isn't wet yet she shivers.
She almost drowned.
Light falls off her side as a coat
Thrown over one shoulder.
She hopes her belongings caught
On a limb. Her money pouch.
The waters rush on.
She busts a branch over her knee.
Spits into the blaze.
It's the swift life and a long walk
To Monkey Run.

10

Fields

for Bruce Weigl

This was nineteen and seventy.
A woman in a yellow dress
Blowing dust off a record by The Doors.

A big gold sun falls under the combine.
The hands are leaving the fields
For their own table and bed.

Men go to the porch
Doing a slow dance, drinking gin
With women they did not bring.

The talcum under her arms is wet,
Beginning to sour.

It was their reunion. Those who didn't attend
Lived too far, lost their invitation
Or their life in the meantime.

A widow took her hose off
And tore a shot from the yearbook,
A boy headed for a touchdown.

The one drafted
With no friends here, doesn't care.

Through the smoke in the corridor
He hears the sargeant yelling Haul ass,
Men scrambling toward a bank,
Water around the loins
Growing sweet and sour,

Sarge yelling Haul ass
Man thinking dusk, Sarah, harvest.

11

The Beautiful Urinals Of Paris

Many husbands are missing tonight.
Ones who drink together to forget
And ones who drink alone and remember.
A drowned man will not reach his doorbell,
The roses waiting on the tables
Are closing their wet eyes,
Trees along the boulevard are going blind from headlights.
The finest houses have turned their back on the Seine.
All the drunk, married men of the rain
Step into the urinals like women
Entering cathedrals.
With their arms around one another
They listen to their love run out with a hiss,
Worship the steam as it rises off the drain.

The Secret Life Of
Musical Instruments

12

Bent Tones

There was a dance at the black school.
In the shot houses people were busy.

A woman washed her boy in a basin, sucking
A cube of ice to get the cool.

The sun drove a man in the ground like a stake.
Before his short breath climbed the kitchen's steps

She skipped down the walk in a clean dress.
Bad meat on the counter. In the sky, broken glass.

When the local hit the trestle everything trembled —
The trees she blew out of, the shiver owl,

Lights next door — With her fast eye
She could see Floyd Little
Changing his shirt for the umpteenth time.

13

Run For The Roses

Like horses
After the bridle comes off
Musicians on break
Want to be left alone.
They want to stand out of doors breathing even.

Like horses
After the bit lets go of the tongue
Musicians lighten up.
When the last set is over
They sweat freely and roll.

Like the mare with the blaze face
The young singer
Blows her bangs out of her eyes.
She doesn't have to be led to her stall.

What is written on mirrors in Louisville —
Another lovely losing streak,
Speaks for the herd.

The blaze face and the songster
Will not hear the past
Knowing how it smells.
So go down
By the dozen
Dead roses of the heart.

14

Crescendo

When the gentle are resting or kissing
In parked cars
The violent get themselves up
Killingly.
I mean to speak of the marked men
Beautiful but bad.
Too often they have been told
To move on and fired
When they come out of the cold buildings
Of the capitols,
Tavern in the hills, house on the plain
And take up with the pale
Insomniacs of love.
These are the crossed women
Sanctified and damned.
Their slips cling
Like shy children.
Their nails are chewed.
And like those of us asleep at the wheel
Or lying down in the seat
Listening to a chain-smoking DJ
Play Bolero
Their mother may have been kind,
Though she claimed she was tired
Of headlines and snowfall,
The absence of light
In the bedroom. O I am talking to you
Black moon. I'm warning you.

15

The Substitute Bassist

During the very rich times of the Duke
The trains, long and slower than funerals
In the Quarter;

Musicians went to their berths like the grave.
They were going home. Rocking.

The bass man stayed up alone
To pay his respects to the moon. He sat
In the draft of her.

Their instruments grew silent and cold
In the lining of their cases.

The hand with the glove on let up the shade.
A ground fog moved alongside the coach.

He drew in the pane
As though carving a scar in the bark,
Willow Weep for Me.

16

Alla Breve Loving

Three people drinking out of the bottle
In the living room.
A cold rain. Quiet as a mirror.

One of the men
Stuffs his handkerchief in his coat.
Climbs the stairs with the girl.
The other man is left sitting

At the desk with the wine and the headache
Turning an old Ellington side
Over in his mind. And over
Like a stone on a bank.

He remembers
When she was his girl.
He held her like a saxophone.
Her tongue trembling at the reed.

The man lying next to her now
Thinks of another woman.
Her white breath idling

Before he drove off.
He said something about a spell
Watching the snow fall on those curls.

The musician
Crawls back into his horn,
Ancient terrapin
At the approach of the wheel.

17

Jazz Impressions In The Garden

Dark as a cow. It's a downpour.
Mud on every sole in the vestibule.
A boy can lean on his oar, drift
Out of this world.
The time has come now
For the cold eyes of the rain and the writer
To bear down. This could be Harlem,
The old theater where they used to lay up
Smoking Kools in the balcony,
Tying off a vein
With something found on the floor,
Or Arkansas, a pair of antlers
Glued to a cedar board.
Which do you want, this or more of the same.
All the great dead lie on their backs
Under grass and granite
Listening to women sing, dragging their chains.
Requiem of the thunder. Roll on.

18

The Secret Life Of Musical Instruments

for Claudia Burson

Between midnight and Reno
The world borders on a dune.
The bus does not stop.

The boys in the band have their heads on the rest.
They dream like so and sos.

The woman smokes
One after another.
She is humming Strange Fruit.
There is smoke in her clothes, her voice,
But her hair never smells.

She blows white petals off her lapel,
Tastes salt.
It is a copacetic moon.

The instruments do not sleep in their dark cribs.
They keep cool, meditate.
They have speech with strangers:

Come all ye faithless
Young and crazy victims of love
Come the lowlife and the highborn
All ye upside down shitasses

Bring your own light
Come in Be lost Be still
If you miss us at home
We'll be on our way to the reckoning.

19

Libretto

Night is dark
On the streets without names.

Men piss in the ditch, on the toe of their shoes
Thinking it must be rain or hail.

The feet of their women swell like a melon.
Their ironing boards bow
Under the weight of beautiful linen
They do for other women.

Radios are turned up to beat thunder.
Translations of the gospel
Back into tongues.

The tiger lilies' tremble.
Bottles get busted, somebody cut.

A man in a black shirt
Gets off the bus with no suitcase,
Leans on his wife. Umbrella
With a broken spoke.

A girl sits out of doors in her slip.
She turns fourteen, twenty-eight, fifty-six,
Goes crazy.

The saxophone plays it for somebody else.
Play hell.

20

Listening To A Brown-Eyed Man
Play It For Somebody Else

An old woman riding the bus folds her paper
    thinking of him.
A man gets out of a government car, shows a boy
    a picture of him.
A woman finishes off a fifth talking about him. Or just
    talking
About the brown eyes.

Somewhere between the bed and the clothesline
You stopped losing blood. The only thing I had to go by,
An envelope that went through the wash.
There were rumors. No one had influenza. There were no
    deer
Left to shoot. People had to do something
With their lives. The women you sold the encyclopedias
Didn't get any volumes after C. She remembers you,
College boy. Working his way through.
Beautiful eyes. The man at the post office
Gave me your combination. When I opened the box
Your sour breath blew in my face. I heard
You went south in a tent. Revivals one night,
Movies for men the next. You hired someone
To wipe off the folding chairs.
You walked throught the parking lot.
Boys were drinking root beer. Setting fire to cars.
They whipped you good. Your landlady
Patched you up. She said you would be back.
You left your felt hat and your albums,
Nothing but blues.
You did time. I heard. Your mother is dead.
The past is a deep place. I know
Lightning doesn't strike lovers or old musicians,
They disappear in a dream of the tree it does.

from Livelihoods Of Freaks
And Poets Of
The Western World

21

from
Livelihoods Of Freaks And
Poets Of The Western World

Franz was washing my back
In the clawfoot tub.
We weren't at his house. Not mine.
In all the rooms of summer and night
We were alone.
I was telling him about Julia Pastrana.
Her burning ugliness,
Beautiful manners. Mercy,
Wasn't it hot.
He had been drinking with a vengeance.
He would not use a washcloth.
His fingers fell on me
Gentle as tears.
I had reached the part where
The man she had made so wealthy
Forbade her going among the people.
The man, don't you see,
Wanted no one to weary
Of her terrible features.
He wanted them to keep paying.
The moon passed unseen. I shivered.
Franz was rubbing my hair dry
With his good shirt.
We sat at the long table. We had fountain pens,
Some more wine. I wrote
Women get light at midnight. He wrote
Men go blind.

22

Blazes
for the ones shaving without a mirror

A man came home with my brothers.
He had on a hunting vest,
A bird losing blood and feathers from the pouch.
I thought of a burning bush.

It was raining again,
Someone driving nails in a board.

I brushed the folds out of the tablecloth.
The visitor stood in the steam
Lifting off the table.
He wiped his hands on my apron.

The voice of my father came on
Gentle as a lamp
A page being turned in its light.

They pushed their plates away, took their chair
    to the front room,
And lit up. I went to mine.
It was a school night. I held my pillow to my chest
And said Kiss me Frankie.

I was old enough
To know love is blind as the old woman
Pulled down the hall by her dog.

Their guns leaned against the wall
But men in those days kept themselves armed
In the dark and rain.

It never stopped.
Everyone who could handle an oar
Headed for hell in a boat.

I thought of a burning bush.

The story not told by the one cooking supper
Was heard by the fire.

23

Yellow Dresses

A woman and her sisters would follow
The bees to their tree.
There was no wind or word
From New Orleans. She wore several yards
Of gauze over her clothes,
Long gloves to pull the comb out of the trunk.
The others lay down in the grass,
Cats in the sunlight,
And the smallest sister would lie
In the lap of the oldest
Until she stroked her hair and spoke.
Close to the swarm, the fine vibration
In her voice, spirit of the hive.

24

Landlocked, Fallen, Unsung
in praise of Agee

Those who went shares, plodded
Through the dust of their life. Like a horse.
A swayback woman would get up
From red dreams, cross an uneven floor
Before the cock on the hood cleared his throat.
In sleep, the man
Hurled another stone at the sun.
The visitor from the North
Pretended not to rouse,
Not watch her
Pull a rag off a hook at the washstand,
Scrub her chest, wipe blood
Between the legs,
Pin her hair up for church
With no mirror.
This was the time
For laying by. He knew. She knew.
He was a shack of a man.
He would cut off his thumbs for her.

25

Obedience Of The Corpse

The midwife puts a rag in the dead woman's hand,
Takes the hairpins out.

She smells apples,
Wonders where she keeps them in the house.
Nothing is under the sink
But a broken sack of potatoes
Growing eyes in the dark.

She hopes the mother's milk is good a while longer,
The woman up the road is still nursing —
But she remembers the neighbor
And the dead woman never got along.

A limb breaks,
She knows it's not the wind.
Somebody needs to set out some poison.

She looks to see if the woman wrote down any names,
Finds a white shirt to wrap the baby in.
It's beautiful she thinks —
Snow nobody has walked on.

26

Clockmaker With Bad Eyes

I close the shop at six. Welcome wind,
Weekend with two suns, night with a travel book,
The dog-eared sheets of a bed
I will not see again.

I not of time, lost in time
Learned from watches —
A second is a killing thing.

Live your life. Your eyes go. Take your body
Out for walks along the waters
Of a cold and loco planet.

Love whatever flows. Cooking smoke, woman's blood,
Tears. Do you hear what I'm telling you?

27

Who Sit Watch In Daylight

A radio comes on in a yellow kitchen.
The woman is dressed
And dreaming up a sweat.
It is not yet seven, but it is hot.

The others are rising.

She feels her heart sweeten.
They come to the table
Join hands and tell what they know.
They leave. So many bees.
She stares at dust falling.

The Gospel Hour has begun.

Her love is getting thick and warm
As honey with the lid off.
She watches the hall. In a moment
The dead man is in the doorway.
He has on the Hawaiian shirt, white slacks.

He glows.

Sunlight pours
Through the chambers of her heart.
They look at one another
As though they were kids.
They had a code.
The singers shout and rock.

She stacks the cereal bowls.
Opens the icebox.
And stares at the cold light.
He looked good in his summer clothes.

28

Boss Of Darkness

If he lived to be forty
He would not work.
He would sit on his cot
Looking at his face in his shoes,
At his hands the blueprint
Of a house he would never move into.
The flies could have his toast.
If he saw the woman at the clothesline
He would not reach under the springs
For the violin.
Everything burned
In the soaked rags of his dreams:
Leaves, bankrupt hotels, letters
From Lily.

29

Fascination

A hotel, speakeasies,
Beautiful and idle boys
Throwing bottles at streetlights.
Beyond them, the trees. A man,
Woman and grown girl
In a house like a closed country.
In the house in the night
A minimum of sound: meal seeping
Through sacks in the pantry,
Hair rinsed out over a basin, a lesson.
Outdoors, the orchestra
Of frogs and bullbats.
The man brought the radio home.
The women turned their backs on the fire.
He tuned. After the programs
He would walk over the hard wood
In his boots to lock up. The woman
Would put her sewing down. The girl
Watched them climb to their bed,
A wet towel on her shoulder.
Rain he heard beating
The bushes. Paint peeling.
She thought of everyone old
Turning their heads in their sleep,
The barn owls
When a moon breaks into their loft.

30

The Night Before The
Sentence Is Carried Out

a woman is riding a bus
With a sack of black apples in her lap.

The bus stalls on the dam.
She pulls a knife out of the sack, throws it
In the water with the blade half open

Like the eyes of a lawyer
Who has been drinking heavy
For a month, more than a month.

He passes out in his boat.
When he comes to, the lake is another man's
Suit, in the billfold
Photo of another man's wife.

The woman waits for everyone to get off
Before she does.
She reaches up to put the pins in her hair.

The condemned man is rubbing his arms
Thinking about someone
He used to be married to.
He reaches under the cot, touches the cold wire.

She stands up brushing her clothes,
The bottom falls out of the sack.
She leaves the apples scattered in the aisle.

31

Smoke Rings

While others are talking someone gets up
And leaves the room.
They are his guests, he is not the host.

In his garden a chair has been planted, a table
With his cards laid out
Face down the way some bury their dead.

He has forgotten which zone he belongs to,
If he is married or still living
Alone like the woman who had on his socks or
A clock that runs behind.

Birds escaping the incinerator.
The stars colder than men
Looking in mirrors.

His friends pull out of the drive,
Their headlights grow dim
As her eyes.

He strokes a moth on the screen,
Goes indoors and sits naked
And whistling the rest of the night.

He opens the cigar box that never loses its smell,
Listens to the wind
Blowing through the trees along the Nile.

32

Wanderer In His Thirtieth Year

Clearly, the stores were closed.
The road open.
Snow blowing up the steps
Like dust. I let him in.
Took his things.
He just wanted to sit
In the dark, watch the fire.
He did not drink
So much as he slept
Not sleep
So much as he dreamed.
He left before I got up.
The Longhair bore her litter
On the fleece of his coat.
One bus groaned
Over the mountain.
Carrying one rider.
Snow whirling over floor
Like dust.

33

Vanish

Because I did not die
I sit in the captain's chair
Going deaf in one ear, blind in the other.
I live because the sea does.

All I remember, three stories
Of rooms:

In one, a girl is sewing a dress
For her brother's funeral.
Jars of rhubarb cool on the porch.
A man puts his music away,
But not the instrument.
The spare room is made up,
The guest wants a lift into town.

A light stumbles in the corridor —
Someone who doesn't know where to go
When the bar shuts down
For blue laws.

Steal away,
Shadows of old boyfriends.

Since that night
Some of us have looked for better lamps
To read by.
Others have worn a soft robe,
Stirred the coals.

Because I did not marry
I wash by the light of the body.
Soap floats out of my mind.
I have almost forgotten
The sailor whose name I did not catch,
His salty tongue on my ear,
A wave on a shell.

34

White Shutters

I was in another room
Reading Pablo's memoirs.
My mother, carrying a sheet up the stairs.
The only friend I could claim at the time
Was sleeping his life away
In a house on a cape.
The window he lay beside
Would not open or close.
The waves kept coming in and going out
Of his eyes same as the women
Who know when someone falls overboard.
They know which is the widow.
I was already swimming past the bed,
Dresser, chair, guitar.
The wind blew through the high ceilings
Of his heart. I am sure
He said, Oh.
I heard one of those women
Touch my shoulder and say, He's gone.
He's gone, she said. I felt old.
That quick, like a girl.
That quiet, a page floating from a book.

35

Water, Blood, And Desire

They sit beside water.
One returning, one saying, So long.
They drink beer and never mention Saigon,
The burning roofs, or names on their tongues.

It is Sunday and there are horses.

Along the fence, a woman wields a sickle.
The honeysuckle smells too sweet.
Bees even after rain.

Sun enough and wind to stir
Her skirt, a dust storm,
Memory that carres a little sting.

The men get up, brush off their trousers,
Walk as far as the truck
And part with a short hug.

She turns down the shed path
Without a wave or a Good luck Soldier.

Sunday and horses.

Tell me now,
Is it the men on the bank, the meadow,
Or the colt who dreams,
Who rolls in the downed vine?

CD Wright was born in 1949 in the Ozark Mountains. She attended college in Tennessee and Arkansas. She has earned a living in Arkansas, Atlanta, New York, and San Francisco as a teacher of writing, as a publisher, and at various less gratifying employment. Wright edits a book press, Lost Roads Publishers, with poet Forrest Gander. She is the recipient of a 1981 Fellowship for Creative Writers from the National Endowment for the Arts, and is currently living in Dolores Hidalgo, Mexico.

MacArthur "Genius" Grant - 2004